Invisible Girl

Emily Smith

BookLeaf Publishing

India | USA | UK

Presentation by *BookLeaf Publishing*

Web: www.bookleafpub.com

E-mail: info@bookleafpub.com

ISBN: 9789360947729

First edition 2024

ACKNOWLEDGEMENT

I would like to thank my life circumstances for bringing me all this inner turmoil, which gave me the need to get it out. I would also like to thank my friends for listening to my inner turmoil and helping me let it go.

PREFACE

2023 was a year of adjustment and change, it required mental shifts and revisions to old patterns and habits. Writing was a way for me to work through my feelings and figure out how to deal with them. This book is a reflection of internal turmoil and emotions, as I allow myself to feel and heal. As I try to figure out myself, understand my past, and grab a hold of my future.

Dream a Little Dream

It was an amazing thing we had,
Those days felt magical.
When we would walk, and talk, and dream,
My heart, it felt so full.

I let myself fall back,
I allowed myself to let go.
This little tiny dream I had,
I allowed that dream to grow.

I felt the strength in our connection,
I felt the sameness in our needs.
I thought we'd chase those dreams we shared,
I thought, together, we'd plant those seeds.

But we did not, in fact,

Hold hands and chase those dreams.
We did not get a chance to see,
Just where those dreams could lead.

I allowed myself to fall into you,
I dreamed a little dream.
I cannot take those feelings back,
They are with me forever now, or so it seems.

The Fire

We met one day with a tiny spark,
That spark turned into a flame.
That flame grew furious and fast,
In like a tornado, it came.

They say flames that burn bright,
Those flames that heat up fast.
They say that those relationships,
Are just not meant to last.

I ignored those worries,
The concerns, the what if's.
I cut out that noise,
I banked on my wish.

I lit my candle,
With our amazing light,
I watched it glow,
Strong, beautiful, and bright.

Then I watched it fade,
But I couldn't understand why.
Our flame grew dim,
Long before it's time.

Our flame got snuffed out,
It did not die.
Our flame was cut short,
Before we really got that chance to try.

It still lingers here,
Our flame inside of my heart.
I feel it dance and light up,
When I remember that amazing start.

That tiny little spark,
That spark that pulled me in.
I'll wish forever and a day,
We could have that back again.

Not Well

I have not been feeling well,
I have not been myself.
We put our relationship in a box,
Now that box is on my shelf.

I wish I could remove that box,
Open it to what is inside.
Respark our amazing connection,
Grow it long, far, and wide.

I would remove it with care,
Tenderness, and concern.
I would light that little flame,
And allow that flame to burn.

Burn bright like a candle,
Or the sun on a hot, hot day.
Let it melt my worries and fears,
Watch them all drip away.

Let our amazing vibration ignite and dance,
As we float across the floor.
Letting it consume ourselves,
Like we never have before.

But I cannot do that right now,
For now is not the time.
I must sit, and be still,
My light pushing hard to shine.

I have not been feeling well,
I have not been myself.
We put our relationship in a box,
Now that box is on my shelf.

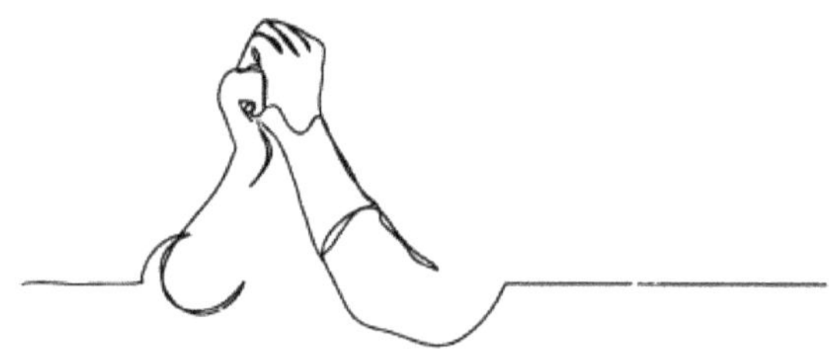

I Dream of Us

I dream of us, sometimes, at night
Sometimes, right in the middle of the day.
I dream of us, and when I do,
I imagine all of the things I would say.

I dream of dancing in the dark,
Your hands around my waist.
I can feel your soft skin, I can feel your rough
hair,
Brushing against my face.

I see little clips of us,
Moments we made together.
I think about them all the time,
Wondering, what happened to forever?

Then I am reminded,
We never actually said that word,
We never even said forever.
Forever? That's absurd!

It's not at all though, it is not absurd,
To feel forever in my heart.
It was an amazing thing I experienced,
I felt forever from the start.

I dream of us sometimes,
I remember all that was there.
I dream of the memories I took with me,
I handle them with care.

Sacrifice

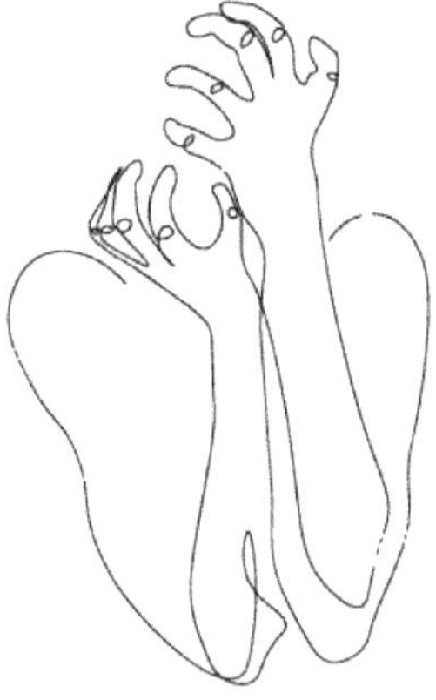

When I think back on all of myself that I've
given,
Not only to you, but every other one before.

I've driven at least a million miles, or more.
I've spent thousands of dollars, out of my
pockets they'd pour.

I've sacrificed feelings, emotions, sanity, and
words,
Listening to you, but never being heard.

I've shown patience, understanding, kindness,
and spirit,
My heart on my sleeve is where I would wear it.

I've lost days, probably weeks, maybe months
upon end,
Beating myself up for things I've done, felt, and
said.

I've cried until I could not shed one more tear,
For losing you was my one biggest fear.

I've broken dishes, screamed out loud, and torn
up pictures in a rage,
Feeling like your pet bird, always kept in a cage.

I've allowed who I am to be altered by men,
Repeating their words in my head, again and
again.

"You're too much, you're too hard, you're too
loud, you're too strong,"
Words to ensure that I do not belong.

I've lost who I am so many times,
Searching for myself in the deep dark confines.

I'm still searching for me, digging through dirt,
Looking for a woman who is stained by hurt.

Wearing sadness and pain, like her heart on her
sleeve,
Awaiting the day I can let go, and breathe.

Noise

There's a battle in my mind,
It's winner takes all.
The good and the bad are taking sides,
They each want the other to fall.

There is so much noise inside my head,
It's screaming, crying, searing pain.
Thoughts of us replaying in my mind,
Again, and again. And again.

The clutter clouds my mind like static tv,
A sound that I cannot turn down.
You can read that static on my face,
It quiets my rainbow of emotions to brown.

I hear laughter, love, and excitement,
As we play together under the sun.
I hear memories we would make and share,
All grand things, now completely done.

I hear the crunch of the leaves beneath our feet,
As we walked for miles on hikes.
Filling our lungs with crisp, fresh air,
Bringing future plans to light.

You would think that time would muffle that
noise,
Once in a while it does.
But then it all comes surging back,
My heart stuck on what once was.

Sit With Me A While

Come sit next to me, let's talk for a while,
Tell me a story from your past.
Enlighten me with things I don't know,
Give me memories that will last.

I like to hear your voice,
Would you sit with me a while.
Could you tell me all the things about myself,
That make you want to smile.

I like to hear you laugh aloud,
As your memories unfold.
A life well lived told through your tales,
Big stories of days grown old.

I think about your days gone by,
It's hard to imagine the things you've seen and
done.
Moments that took your breath away,
When you stood your ground, and didn't run.

I hear a life of struggles, grief, and labor,
A strong being with a powerful soul.
To be trapped inside that deep echoing cave,
Showing such patience and self control.

I also hear the joy in there,
Recollections that measure the space you have
traveled,
Pockets of timeless treasures,
Amid the seams that have since unraveled.

Talk to me until it gets dark,
Let the stars come out to smile.
Come, sit down next to me,
Let's talk for a while.

In My Head

Was this all in my head?
Did I make this all up?
Were there memories here?
Did you fill up my cup?

In another life, we did these things,
Imperfect, soft, and true.
We stumbled, we fell, and we caught ourselves,
Together we made it through.

I have built an entire life in my head,
A fantasy of you and me.
A kingdom of treasures, a sea of misfortune,
I live in a land of make believe.

I'm up in the clouds,
Drifting through dreams.
Trudging through dark places,
That's my reality, It seems.

Keep Growing

Can you stay standing tall,
In the dark of the night?
When the wind blows cold,
And shade covers the light.

Can you maintain your strength
When you can't see ahead?
When there are no answers to offer,
Only possibilities to dread.

Can you cut through that darkness,
And see that small glow?
A flicker so small,
You might call it hope.

Then in like a flash,
Hope tears open that glow.
Revealing a light
that continues to grow.

Like a flower in spring,
Hope blooms, constant and clear.
It needs rest, it needs rain,
To make beauty appear.

Beauty we name as

Experiences and lessons,
That open our heart,
and soften our expressions.

During every single season of our lives,
We are steadily growing.
Continually adding to our collection
Of learning and knowing.

Some seasons are short,
Some seasons are long.
Some seasons can be condensed
Into a three minute song.

All molding and forming
The person that is you.
Stay consistent, stay clear,
Stay strong, stay true.

Pieces of Grief

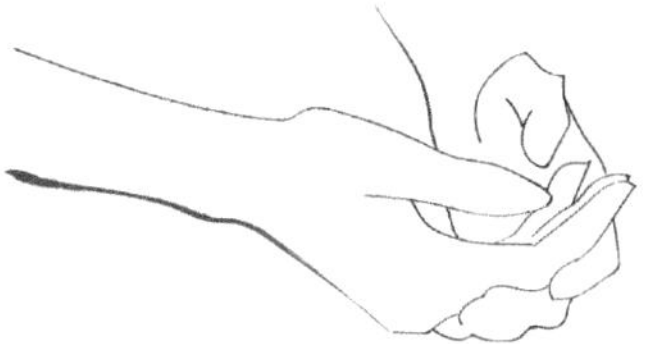

I'll take your pain,
Give it all to me.
Let your heart and your mind
Run wild, far, and free.

I'm familiar with pain,
It feels at home here.
With its two best friends,
Worry and fear.

Wrestling with grief
Is a pathway unprepared,
Not one we give as gifts,
But one that's often shared.

Each entity experiences
Grief their own way.
Unfamiliar with this visitor,
Or how long they will stay.

The weight of our sorrow,
Heavy and dense,
It limits our joy,
Chips away at common sense.

Allowing our hearts to drag
Down with our spirit.
Digging into the ground,
So far down we can't feel it.

A slow droop in our posture,
A noticeable quiet in our voice.
Torment so deep we don't
Feel it's our choice.

To push back against
The sorrow and pain.
Wishing it gone,
Never returning again.

We cannot avoid
The mess it creates,
As we pick up our pieces,
We see it's altered our shapes.

As they come back together,
We see they're no longer the same.
Our pieces have changed,
Throughout life's immense game.

It Was Real

The places I've gone,
The things that I've seen,
I must remind myself,
It was not just a dream.

The steps that I've taken,
The journey I've made,
Such memories kept dear,
Never to trade.

The smells, sights, and sounds,
The things that I've felt,
Those things were so real,
Upon my memories they melt.

Good things were here,
Right here in this life,
Lighting little fires,
In the depth of sorrow and strife.

Through searching and stumbling,
There were times I'd stand tall, strong, and proud.
I'd feel so damn good,
I lived life out loud.

Perhaps that is the lesson,
When we're down, and we're blue.
Our lives were worth living,
We did make it through.

You

You feel like love,
You feel like home,
You make me feel like I'm never alone.

You make me whole,
You make me strong,
You make me feel like you're where I belong.

You make me happy,
You make me smile,
You make the world disappear for a while.

You make me question,
You make me think,
You make me float when my strength wants to sink.

You keep it real,
You keep it light,
You keep it grounded with your strength and your might.

You opened the door,
You took the first step,
You were the reason this feeling was kept.

You closed the door,
You took the key,
Now there is nothing left here but me.

Invisible Girl

Invisible girl walks into a room,
Walks straight to the back,
Sits alone in a booth.

Invisible girl watches couples on dates,
Watches waiters take orders,
And deliver the plates.

Invisible girl smells the food in the air,
Hears the clink of the glasses,
As celebrations are shared.

Invisible girl shares no words as she eats,
Enjoys no discussions,
Only shares empty seats.

Invisible girl stays at her table when she's done,
Watching families around her,
Making memories and having fun.

Invisible girl takes care of the bill on her own,
Living life solo,
Is all she's ever known.

Invisible girl stays just a little while longer,

Knowing when she goes home,
The loneliness grows stronger.

Invisible girl walks into a room,
You wouldn't know she was here,
If I hadn't told you.

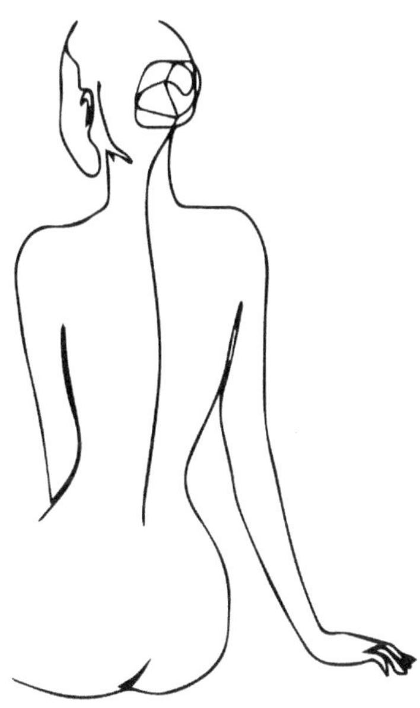

Our Story

There was a time when I had hoped,
That you would be my last.
Now, when I think about you,
Your words are written in my past.

No longer future tense for us,
Our story goes untold.
Adventures, dramas, suspense stories;
Never to unfold.

Our story is woefully short,
But oh, so very sweet.
The strong connection with you,
Felt substantial and elite.

Only a short chapter in a grand novel,
There are no answers to find.
Simply fantasies and dreams,
Of a love story of mine.

As I turn the page of this last chapter,
You're no longer in the story.
I'll have to write this next leg alone,
On life's big unknown journey.

Convenient Love

Love as a convenience,
Like a little corner store.
Always right around the corner,
Always there if you need more.

But love as a convenience
Is not the best you've ever had.
It's love that fits your needs right now,
Not necessarily good, not necessarily bad.

It's love that asks for effort,
That makes love worth your time.
Love that goes through ups and downs,
And always makes the climb.

Love that bends but doesn't break,
Love that stretches far and wide.
Love that returns each and every day,
As the ocean brings the tide.

Love that has a strong foundation,
Built upon trust and understanding.
Love that offers a gentle home,
That welcomes you to a soft landing.

Love as a convenience,
Can be an easy thing to score.
But love that you have worked to hold,
You'll find is worth much more.

A Gift

Does calling pain a gift,
Make it an easier pill to swallow?
Does all the pain and suffering,
Make for a better tomorrow?

Yes it's true, we can learn and grow,
From the capsized tide.
But that certainly does not make
It all feel ok inside.

Some call it a lesson,
You call it a blessing.
I do believe life was meant
To keep you guessing.

But a 'gift', no,
Your pain is not a gift.
Gifts are happy little treasures,
Gifts bring smiles, they uplift.

We may grow from our pain,
We will definitely learn.
But nothing feels good,
In the midst of the slow, fiery burn.

Pain can sometimes stay the night,
But please be gone when I wake up.
Pain has never once stopped by,
To help fill up your cup.

So when your body feels like nothing's there,
When you're empty and you're hollow,
Does calling pain a 'gift',
Make it an easier pill to swallow?

The Key

I am fearful of my future,
For I know not what it holds.
An unknown story comes to me,
Slowly, it unfolds.

Past misgivings have my stomach,
All tied up in knots.
For I cannot depend on the frivolity
Of luck to call the shots.

You plan your life out in your head,
So strategically.
But when those milestones are not met,
It's like you've lost the key.

Your life no longer a familiar place,
Lost from the path you made.
You'll make it back, oh yes you will,
Just might not be today.

Close your eyes and hold your breath,
And take that first scary step.
Into the darkness of the future,
Where unknown ecstasy is kept.

For yes, the future holds some things
We may not want to see.
But you will find the most glorious things,
I bet you'll even find that key.

35

Like a Hawk

Move silently, like a hawk,
Don't let them know your next move.
Wait until you're back on top,
Perfectly in your groove.

We women can move mountains,
When we're called to do what's right.
We sharpen our swords, repair our arrows,
Standing stoic, we're here to fight.

Knee deep in the mud,
We'll still pull ourselves out.
Amidst the gossip and the lies,
Through the rumors and the doubt.

We are powerful little stars,
That others try to keep small.
But we rise like the sun each morning,
Standing confident and tall.

So stealthily I move,
Like a hawk zoning in on prey.
Diverting and narrowing my focus,
To create the woman I am today.

Close That Door

You will never know,
Just what you did to me.
You left marks so deep inside
That you could never see.

And I know that
You did not do this willfully.
But you created a hole in my heart
The size of the Caspian Sea.

Like a thief you stole my joy,
Security, trust, and shine.
You took the things you gave to me,
You took things that were mine.

You drew those things away from me,
A way to stay protected.
I was taking down a wall,
While you hid and deflected.

Yes I know there was distance,
And that long drive is hard.
Love doesn't feel quite the same,
Sent by mail, in a card.

But I would have powered through that
Burdensome, grueling distance.
I would have continued trying,
I would have been the resistance.

I would have waited five years for you,
I'd swim the deepest sea.
But I had to stop and ask myself,
Would you do the same for me?

When time is of the essence,
When your heart cannot wait anymore.
When you feel you've finally had enough,
It's time to close that door.

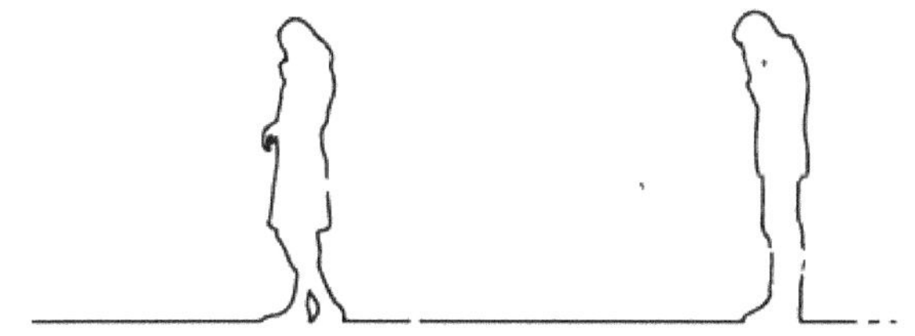

Keep Going

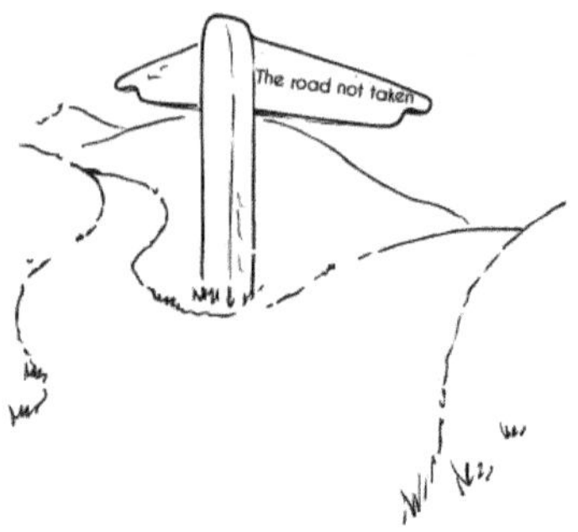

Continue walking,
Move on ahead.
There's more to see,
More paths to tread.

More lessons to learn,
Adventures to make,
Sunsets to see,
Pictures to take.

Better choices abound,
Kinder love to seek.
Never settling,
Don't take that seat.

Ahead unknown,

The world awaits.
A journey unfolds,
Our life it creates.

Inch by inch,
Mile by mile.
We will get there,
Might take a while.

Return to You

Sometimes we find ourselves content
To push aside our needs.
Extending ourselves well beyond
Our clear abilities.

Giving more and more away,
Until there's nothing left.
Looking back at our reflections,
We find ourselves bereft.

Our kindness only something
We tend to give to others.
We give away so very much,
It bleeds away our colors.

Never flipping the mirror around,
Giving kindness to ourselves.
Only piecing it away,
Until we're nothing more than shells.

The shells of stars that shone so bright,
You could see it with closed eyes.
Stars that fill the darkness,
And illuminate the skies.

Return to you, go find yourself
Hidden deep within your soul.
Bring back that glowing star for us,
The one that shines like gold.

Dance

Each morning the sun breaks the horizon
And provides us a new beginning.
Never once asking us,
If we're losing or we're winning.

For to greet each day
With our eyes open wide,
Is the true essence of
A grand winning prize.

The ability to begin again,
The chance to start anew.
A promise we make to ourselves,
The universe pulls it through.

To change the things,
To right our wrong doing.
The opportunity to dig deeper,
And continue pursuing.

Each day brings new hope,
If we're given that chance,
To make beauty in every moment,
And find time to dance.

We cannot see what's in front of us,
And we cannot hold onto our past.
We can only grab onto what's here right now,
Knowing full well, it won't last.

Not My Place

A place you don't belong
Ties your stomach up in knots.
You'll find fear and discomfort
Run away with your thoughts.

In a room full of people,
You feel entirely alone.
This is not my place,
This does not feel like home.

These are not my people,
They do not care for me.
They don't understand my feelings,
They don't see what I see.

A room full of people,
To whom I cannot relate.
A place to talk, but not understand,
A place to argue, but not debate.

Chill sets into your bones,
Quiet takes over your voice.
A place of no connection,
A place that's full of noise.

No sense of belonging here,
I cannot spread my wings.
I need a space where songs are heard,
A space where my heart sings.

Onward and upward we go,
Until we've reached the top.
A place that feels like home,
And welcomes you to stop.

Broken

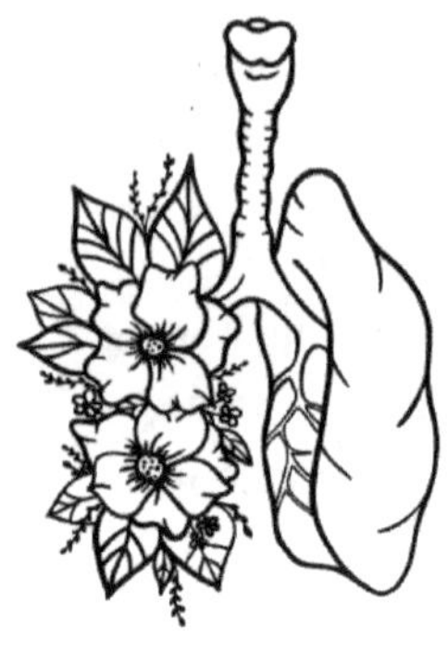

Maybe I am broken,
But you are broken too.
I just happen to be broken
In different ways than you.

My heart's a little battered,
My trust's a little rusty.
Your feelings have been trampled,
Your light's a little dusty.

Together we could do this,
Repair each others' wounds.
Fill each others cups,
Create a life we both consume.

Those cracks and bumps and bruises,
All receipts from people we've been.
You don't have to return a thing,
But you can begin again.

www.ingramcontent.com/pod-product-compliance
Lightning Source LLC
LaVergne TN
LVHW050937200726
843508LV00011B/2368